T0277831

IMAGES
of America

FOREST LAKE

The Forest Lake water tower had been a familiar landmark since it was built in 1921 by the Minneapolis Steel and Machinery Company. Some residents called it the "symbol of home," as one could always spot the tower from off in the distance and know that home was just up ahead. Boaters and snowmobilers used it as a beacon for finding their way back to town. During World War II, a siren at the top signaled blackout warnings and sounded the end of the war. It alerted volunteer firemen about fires, drownings, and approaching tornados and even told the youngsters when it was time to go home. The tower later fell into disrepair, and efforts to save the beloved "Tin Man" were unsuccessful. When the city council voted to have it removed, many citizens were outraged, as it represented one of the last landmarks the city had. It met its end on November 9, 2006. (Courtesy of the Forest Lake Historical Society.)

ON THE COVER: Back in the early days of the bathing beach, crowds would gather in the lake to cool off during the hot summer months. The shallow waters of First Lake provided a large and safe swimming area for children to play. Boats could be rented from Boehm's Boat Landing for the day. Here, children enjoy an afternoon of lake activities. (Courtesy of the Forest Lake Historical Society.)

IMAGES
of America

FOREST LAKE

Justin Brink

ARCADIA
PUBLISHING

Copyright © 2023 by Justin Brink
ISBN 978-1-4671-6025-4

Published by Arcadia Publishing
Charleston, South Carolina

Printed in the United States of America

Library of Congress Control Number: 2023937805

For all general information, please contact Arcadia Publishing:
Telephone 843-853-2070
Fax 843-853-0044
E-mail sales@arcadiapublishing.com

Visit us on the Internet at www.arcadiapublishing.com

CONTENTS

Acknowledgments

In planning for the Diamond Jubilee celebration in 1949, townspeople were asked to bring historical items from home that could be put on display for all to enjoy. That request was met tenfold. It was at this time when the idea of a historical society was first discussed. Many of the artifacts present had already been passed down a generation or two and might soon be lost in the years to come. Sadly, the society never came to fruition. In the ensuing years, a few history-minded citizens decided to preserve what they could from the living memories of their elders, essentially creating a historical society within themselves. Elsie Vogel, an early Forest Lake transplant from Finlayson, created a historical series for the *Forest Lake Times* called Reflections. These articles captured the feel-good memories of days gone by and helped establish a historical record of the town's history. Forest Lake is indebted for her work. Norman and Beulah (Engquist) Tolzmann could be described as "lighthouse keepers" for Forest Lake. Their interest in local history was evident by all who knew them. Both were advocates for historical preservation, and many artifacts of Forest Lake's past survive today due to their efforts. Brian Tolzmann, a nephew of Norman and Beulah, carries on the penchant for area history like none other. Aside from his successful work in broadcasting, Brian is a research behemoth, having consulted for the publishing and entertainment industries as well as contributing to many books and Public Broadcasting Service documentaries. His knowledge of the local and often unknown history has provided this author many hours of enjoyment. As we both share a dedication to the accuracy of the historical narrative, no other person was sufficient to give this book its final review, which he provided. I thank Brian for being an ongoing resource and history colleague.

INTRODUCTION

Like many towns in Minnesota, Forest Lake took its name from the nearby lake; its size and number of trees surrounding it seemed like a natural choice. Then again, it could have been an attempt to make the town sound better than it was, as it needed an enticing name to attract more settlers. The fact was, a considerable amount of Forest Lake at the time was swampland. Even as late as 1909, a prospective farmer wrote home stating, "There is lots of swampy land around here for $25 and up, but it is not worth having." Settlers of the day told stories of Native Americans paddling canoes straight through town, arriving on a small island at the north end to camp for the summer.

Before European settlement, the area between Forest Lake and the town of Wyoming, Minnesota, was a dividing line between the Oceti Ŝakowiŋ to the south (known at the time as the Sioux) and the Ojibwa (or Chippewa) to the north. This line was established by the US government in 1825 under the First Treaty of Prairie du Chien as a means to mitigate intertribal warfare. This and subsequent treaties also pressured Native American leaders to relinquish these territories. Under Article 5 of the treaty, the boundary line passed "between two lakes called by the Chippewas 'Green Lakes' and by the Sioux 'the lakes they bury the Eagles in.' " In this sense, the two lakes were known by their collective name and not individually.

As European settlers arrived from the East in the 1850s, they erected sod and log homes and did their level best to cultivate the land and provide sustenance to their families. In 1868, a railroad was built through Forest Lake and with it came trade, business, and tourists. The town was platted the following year. By the time the township was officially formed in 1874, wood-frame houses were replacing the old sod homes. Hotels and general stores sprang up as well as entrepreneurs wanting to take advantage of what the lake had to offer.

More importantly, town officers and residents alike recognized the need for long-term sustainability and went right to work erecting roads and a new grade school where annual meetings would be held until a town hall was built in 1887. A constable was hired to keep order, and a health officer was paid in 1893 to make a "thorough sanitary inspection of the entire township." Officer Gund Brandt was happy to report the overall sanitary condition to be "excellent . . . without a single case of sickness among man or beast."

The year 1893 also saw the incorporation of the village. A petition was brought to the Board of County Commissioners of Washington County and at 9:00 a.m. on July 10, 1893, the election commenced at J.L. Simmons's store. Election inspectors oversaw the day's proceedings and closed the voting at 5:00 p.m. All voters were in favor for incorporation, and the certification was signed by the county the following day. It was a ray of sunshine in a week that started out gloomy. A day before the election, a gang of thieves robbed the C.V. Smith saloon and patrons at gunpoint and then proceeded to rob several cottages in town.

The turn of the 20th century saw Forest Lake come into its own as a resort town. By the 1920s, rental cabins dotted the shores of all three lakes, with resort owners offering all the trappings of simple lake living. The ability to eschew the busyness of daily life is what attracted the endless summer tourists from the cities, despite foregoing the luxury of indoor plumbing. Forest Lake's rural setting also offered an inconspicuous existence for gangsters who needed to lie low for a time. George "Bugs" Moran had a hideout here in the 1930s as well as the Barker-Karpis Gang—all undercover but in relatively plain sight.

Throughout the mid-20th century, the resort boom continued, until it was met with an adversary that would blight many small towns along the railroad. The Federal-Aid Highway Act of 1956 created an efficient road system to take travelers from one destination to another at greater speeds in shorter amounts of time. This meant that small towns like Forest Lake were bypassed for bigger cities like Duluth, limiting stops to local business. A system designed to connect America came at the cost of dividing it. Thankfully, Forest Lake persevered.

Today, townhomes, condos, and single-family homes dominate the old farming community. The resorts are long gone; only a few cabins remain as vestiges of a time in history that will never be known again. It is indeed regrettable that more effort was not taken to save what is now lost. Aside from the natural occurrence of fires, tornados, etc., there were many landmarks that were taken due to simple indifference or apathy. However, in the last decade, there has been a resurgence in historic preservation. What this could look like for Forest Lake remains to be seen, but there is plenty of history out there worth saving.

Lastly, it is worth noting that every effort was made regarding historical accuracy. Where ambiguity prevailed, an estimate was provided instead of a guess, or it was simply left out. Names of people and places change over time and may not reflect the familiar spelling. Photographs of particular people or locations were chosen based on what the author was able to find from the Forest Lake Historical Society's personal collections, other local societies, or borrowed from the general public. As an example, no photographs could be found of the old Baptist church on South Shore Drive. To borrow a line from Elsie Vogel's book *Reflections* in 1993: "The writing process was not a prejudiced one, only a practical reality."

Both current and former Forest Lake residents are encouraged to reach out to the Forest Lake Historical Society by way of email at forestlakehistory@gmail.com if they have old photographs that could be digitized or donated. The society is happy to scan photographs in cases where a donation is not desired. This allows images like the ones in this book to be shared with others while being kept in the family.

One

THE EARLY YEARS

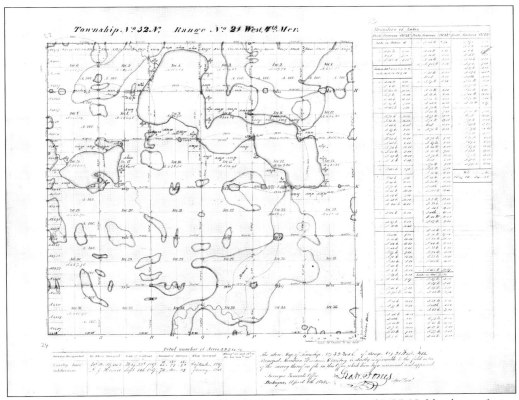

The rectangular survey system was enacted by the Land Ordinance Act of 1785. Unlike the confusing metes and bounds, this system established north-south meridians and east-west base lines. Each township was comprised of 36 sections and was six miles square. This survey was completed in 1848—one of the earliest for this area—and shows just how extensive the water and swampland was at the time. (Courtesy of the Bureau of Land Management, General Land Office.)

This document is the First Treaty of Prairie du Chien, signed on August 19, 1825, in Prairie du Chien, Wisconsin, between the United States and representatives of the Sioux, Sac and Fox, Menominee, Ioway, Winnebago, and Anishinaabeg tribes. Article 5 references Forest Lake in the original names among the Chippewa and Sioux. (Courtesy of the Library of Congress.)

This lithograph of the signing of the First Treaty of Prairie du Chien was drawn by James Otto Lewis and depicts a fanciful view of the day. Although the treaty established the intended boundaries, it did little but to serve as land cession boundaries in later treaties. (Courtesy of the Smithsonian American Art Museum.)

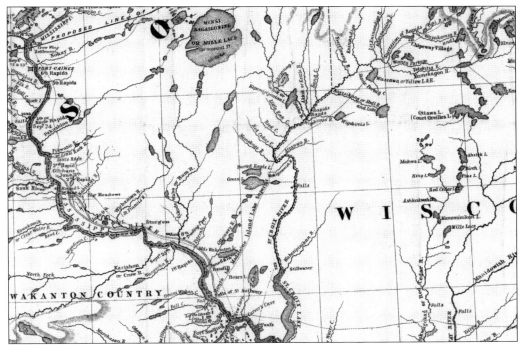

In the center of this partial map from 1844 are the two lakes referenced in the Treaty of Prairie du Chien. Note how the two names were mistakenly transposed. It is also likely that "Buried Eagle L." was the cartographer's shortcut of fitting the original name on the map. (Courtesy of the David Rumsey Historical Map Collection.)

This partial 1852 map by J. Calvin Smith is possibly the first to conclusively identify Forest Lake as well as its location within the boundary of Washington County, created in 1849. Until 1874, Forest Lake was part of Marine Township; it is labeled as "Marine Mills" at upper right on this map. (Courtesy of the David Rumsey Historical Map Collection.)

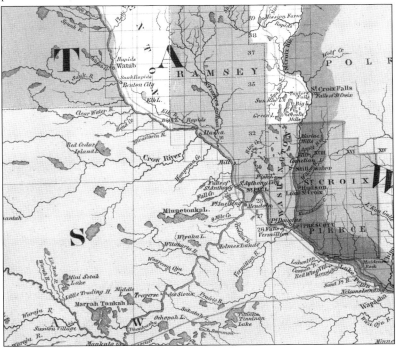

Joseph Lincoln Simmons was born in Forest Lake in 1865 to George and Rebecca (Poston) Simmons. One of Forest Lake's well-known businessmen, he opened his dry goods store in the 1890s, which was a fixture in town for many years. It operates today as Rolseth Drug. The point of land he owned, which separates Second and Third Lakes, is still referred to as Simmons Point. (Courtesy of LoraLee Briley.)

Rose Angela Rahm was born in Columbia, Illinois, in 1872 to Gotthard and Marie (Schneckenburger) Rahm. Seven years his junior, Rose married J.L. Simmons in 1891 at the age of 18. They had three children: George, Lawrence, and Marie. Like many women of the period, very little about her is recorded in history books. (Courtesy of LoraLee Briley.)

This home at 520 North Shore Drive belonged to J.L. and Rose (Rahm) Simmons. This picturesque homestead was certainly not the norm in the 1890s, with its ornate porch and bay window. Many years later, the house was relocated to the southwest neighborhood of Forest Lake. (Courtesy of LoraLee Briley.)

Horses Hugo and Cassius pull a reaper-binder through the field with Eugene Rahm sitting on the back. These early, horse-drawn binders used the traction of being pulled forward to create the rotational force of the wheel. The crops were then cut and bound into sheaves. These reapers were used well into the 20th century and could replace the laborious work of using a scythe. (Courtesy of LoraLee Briley.)

Sitting on a biscuit crate is Gotthard Rahm, wearing a contemplative look on his face. He was born about 1828 in Switzerland, immigrating to Columbia, Illinois, in the 1860s. He married Marie Schneckenburger in 1867 and had three children there before finally settling in Forest Lake around 1875. He served the town in many capacities, including election clerk, treasurer, and supervisor. The Rahm homestead sat on approximately 150 acres that abutted the northwest corner of First Lake and included the outlet of the Sunrise River. The rugged existence of farming life is clearly seen here, given the fact Rahm is only in his 60s. Tragedy seemed to follow the Rahm family throughout their lives in Forest Lake. In 1879, Gotthard broke through the ice and lost his team of horses. Several years later, his son survived a stabbing, and two other children nearly drowned in the lake. In 1896, son Adolph drowned in the Ohio River. Overwhelmed by grief, Gotthard died the following spring by suicide—stabbing himself multiple times in the chest. (Courtesy of LoraLee Briley.)

Ole Alm was a native of Sweden who opened one of the earliest general stores in Forest Lake around 1874. He sold the business in 1877 to John Koller, who ran it for several years. What became of this early business has been lost to history. Alm became a widower early in life but remarried, producing many children. He died in 1899 in Portland, Oregon. (Courtesy of Faith Lutheran Church.)

Olaf Johan Hendrickson emigrated from Sweden in 1877 and settled in nearby Stillwater, Minnesota, as a blacksmith for the state prison. A short time later, he arrived in Forest Lake and took up his trade. Like Ole Alm, he was one of the founders of the Swedish Evangelical Lutheran Church, built in 1888. (Courtesy of Faith Lutheran Church.)

This two-story log house was built around 1856 and served as the home for Jeremiah and Mary (Cartwright) Poston and their 11 children. The home was also used as the earliest schoolhouse, Mary having been a teacher in the area as early as 1859. The school was known as a "vocal" or "blab" school, where children loudly repeated back their teacher's oral lessons. All the noise coming from the school sounded like "blab-blab-blab," hence the name. Because paper was scarce, slate boards and chalk were used, and the teacher only had one or two books to teach from. The first primary school to be built in Forest Lake was in 1874. Rural schools soon sprung up in other parts of town, later consolidating into the school system recognized today. (Courtesy of the Minnesota Historical Society.)

Two

A Village is Formed

The Lake Superior & Mississippi Railroad came through Forest Lake in the fall of 1868. A depot was constructed the following year just north of Broadway Avenue. Its successor, seen here, was erected on the south side. In the fall of 1893, work began on designing the new park, which would be a gathering place for generations of citizens. (Courtesy of the Forest Lake Historical Society.)

Forest Lake was once part of Marine Township. This 1874 map shows the exact year Forest Lake was separated from Marine and became its own village. It also depicts how rural the town used to be, with a single road entering from neighboring Columbus and making its way north into Wyoming. The railroad tracks had been laid a few years earlier, bringing in the necessary business

the new town needed to thrive. The small, darkened square represents the property owned by the Lake Superior & Mississippi Railroad. Land for settlement had been available for nearly 20 years by this time. Still, only 18 families resided within the town. This map also includes the only known example of Clear Lake with the name "Walrus Lake." (Courtesy of the Forest Lake Historical Society.)

The Euclid was a large hotel and resort just off the railroad tracks north of town. It began as the Hotel Leon and boasted "thirty-five bedrooms and six private living rooms." By chance, this photograph happened to capture the new owners of the *Forest Lake Advertiser*, Frank and Homer Wilson (first and second from left), who were boarding at the hotel. (Courtesy of the Forest Lake Historical Society.)

The Forest View Hotel had a somber beginning when it caught fire in 1899 and burned to the ground. It was soon rebuilt, with rooms rented upstairs and a saloon, Phil's Place, on the main floor. This building later became the Park Hotel, Hendrickson's Café, Vogel's Café, and finally, Vogel's Supper Club. Coincidentally, it was lost to fire in 1962. (Courtesy of Bert and Elsie Vogel family.)

Michael Marsh was one of the earliest businessmen in Forest Lake. His grocery store was built next to Clear Lake in 1867. Although it was destroyed by fire the following June, Marsh was undeterred and decided to build a hotel instead. The North Shore House, as it was originally called, was modest and contained six rooms, a kitchen, a dining room, and a sitting area. It was later expanded to include a bar, office, and more rooms. A small general store was added as well, to avoid trips to Wyoming. Marsh was also the town's first postmaster, and the post office was conveniently located in his hotel. At some point, the name changed from the North Shore House to the Marsh Hotel. By this time, the hotel had expanded so much it included 75 guest rooms and several outbuildings. Marsh even had a boat built in 1887 for pleasure cruises around the lake and called it the *Germania*. With a flat bottom, it floated in just 18 inches of water and carried up to 100 passengers. (Courtesy of Washington County Historical Society.)

The hotel and grounds can be seen on full display in this 1890 photograph. Michael Marsh (right) chats with a man said to be named Thurlow, who ran a greenhouse in town just west of the railroad tracks. The flowers in the back of the wagon are being taken to the estate of Gov. William R. Merriam. The hotel rates for that year were $2 per day or $10 per week. Children under 11 and servants were $5 per week. Adjusted for inflation, a week's stay at the Marsh Hotel for a family of four would run approximately $1,000. Guests came from all parts of the country, as evidenced by the hotel register. Pres. Grover Cleveland and First Lady Frances Cleveland also stayed there in October 1887. Michael Marsh eventually became ill and died in 1891. C.T. McNamara purchased the property and continued to operate the hotel until it burned in August 1893. A carriage house survived and is now a residence. (Courtesy of the Forest Lake Historical Society.)

Despite the amount of water that covered the town, there were still plenty of trees to be cut. Forest Lake even had a sawmill at the present-day junction of Highway 97 and July Avenue. The location of this photograph is yet to be determined, but it was probably taken around 1910. (Courtesy of Faith Lutheran Church.)

Lillian Hehner is sitting third from right at this evening dinner party around 1907. Her son Hugh is sitting to her right. Hugh eventually became Forest Lake's first chiropractor, albeit for a short time. Gatherings such as these were common during the spring and summer months, especially with a lot of guests. (Courtesy of Diane Knutson.)

Blacksmith Dennis Cyr and assistant Frank Tourville are working at the bench. Cyr emigrated from New Brunswick, Canada, in 1901. After a brief stint as a farmer in nearby Hugo, he moved to Forest Lake and took up his trade. Of French-Canadian descent, he could only read and write in French until gaining a working knowledge of English. By the time Cyr arrived, two blacksmiths had already preceded him, Alfred King and Oscar Berggren. As a blacksmith, Cyr developed his craft over time, making metal tools, fixing broken wagon parts, and working with horses daily. This allowed him the opportunity to solve a problem at the nearby wire grass camps: horses sinking into the soft ground. He developed bog shoes using a square plank of wood with straps for the hooves to fit into. Later, Cyr turned to woodworking and was adept at making inlaid tables and lamps and even boats and bobsleds. (Courtesy of Patty O'Gorman.)

Forest Lake had no lack of Swedish settlers, and the Engquist brothers were happy to add to their number. John Edward was the first brother to arrive from Sundals-Ryr parish in 1876. He married Sophie Haynes and had nine children. His son William Frederick operated one of the earliest hardware stores in Forest Lake for many years. (Courtesy of Faith Lutheran Church.)

The Engquist home was typical of what many settlers lived in during the 19th century. It was built with logs and covered with clapboards; a kitchen appears to have been added later, to the right. John Edward and his wife were founding members of the Swedish Lutheran Church. Ironically, the homestead was located where St. Peter's Catholic Church and Beltz Park are today. (Courtesy of Faith Lutheran Church.)

Henry Dwight Gurney was a land speculator and real estate dealer. He was one of Forest Lake's early investors, having bought land as early as 1856. He is most known for his summer hotel built on the southwest corner of First Lake. At the time of his death, his real estate holdings across Minnesota totaled $500,000 in value; the equivalent of about $15 million today. (Courtesy of Washington County Historical Society.)

Adeline Paquette was a native of Paris, France, who came to St. Paul in the 1860s and worked as a dressmaker for several years. She married Henry Gurney in 1878 and had a son, Henry Dwight Forest Gurney, later that year. Adeline maintained ownership of the estate in Forest Lake until she died. Her daughter Frances turned the residence into a summer home. (Courtesy of Washington County Historical Society.)

One of the earliest photographs of Forest Lake is shown here at the Gurney resort in 1879. Run by St. Paulite John J. Sloan, it included picnic grounds, rowboats, sailboats, and accommodations for up to 50 guests. At the time, its only rival was Michael Marsh's hotel on the north end of town. Although the Gurneys lived in St. Paul, they often came up to enjoy the resort. The man sitting at left is believed to be H.D. Gurney. Although Gurney owned land all over Minnesota, his resort land was specifically contested by St. Paul lawyers J.B. Olivier and H.B. Farwell. Shortly after they took Gurney to court, he became gravely ill. Judge Crosby went up to the resort so the trial could continue, but it was too late. After Gurney died in 1891, the judge ruled the land to be owned by Olivier and Farwell. Because of the upkeep and improvements to the land, they were ordered to pay Gurney's widow $1,280. She lived there for the rest of her life. (Courtesy of Washington County Historical Society.)

Charlotta "Lottie" Alm was born in Sweden in 1840. She arrived in New York in 1869 and settled in Marine Township (not yet called Forest Lake) a short time later. She and Jonas Johnson were married there in 1871 and had six children. Lottie was a midwife and known for giving her time in helping the sick. The family had a farm just off the northwest corner of Castlewood Golf Course. (Courtesy of Diane Knutson.)

Kirke Eugene Lathrop moved to Forest Lake in 1901 with the Ben Long family and settled in the southwest corner of Forest Lake. This Victorian-style home was certainly impressive for the time, with its three fireplaces and manicured yard. The home and farm were later sold to the George and Mabel Taylor family; it is still a farm today. (Courtesy of the Minnesota Historical Society.)

This view of North Lake Street is one of the earliest known, taken around 1905. The west side was hardly developed at this point, and most of the brick buildings on the right had been constructed within the past several years. At far left is the Walker and Goodine Lumber Yard, started in 1894. This eventually became J.B. Weisser Lumber Company, followed by Salzer Lumber Company. At far right is the Belanger Restaurant, operated by Emma Belanger. She opened the business shortly after 1900 as a saloon, which eventually became a restaurant by the time this photograph was taken. John Lehecka purchased the property and moved the house back toward the lake in the late 1930s so he could build a three-store commercial property in its spot. In February 1955, the house was moved again across the lake to its current site in the southeast neighborhood of Forest Lake. (Courtesy of the Forest Lake Historical Society.)

Andrew W. Johnson built his general store and farm machinery shop in 1902. He sold everything from cornflakes to shoe polish. The store was on the west side of North Lake Street, where the two-story commercial building is today. From left to right are William Pulver, Frank Walker, A.W. Johnson, unidentified, and Otto Johnson. (Courtesy of Washington County Historical Society.)

A.W. Johnson is sitting at left in his general store. His son Rollin is the boy standing closest to him; the others are unidentified. Familiar labels are Morton's Salt, Van Camps Pork & Beans, and Crisco. This area was plagued by fires in the early years. Much of Johnson's store was lost in a fire in March 1910. (Courtesy of Washington County Historical Society.)

Joseph Reioux (left) and Albert Johnson stand behind the counter of their meat market on North Lake Street in 1909. Both men were Forest Lake natives and grew up as farmers until they opened their shop around 1904. Johnson's 6-foot, 3-inch frame may have been imposing at the time, but it served him well for the job. Working hours were long and hard, and endurance was needed for prepping the meat after slaughter to sell to customers. In the foreground, there appears to be enough bacon to feed an army. Everything else not being prepped was stored in the meat cooler at the rear of the store. Signs hanging on the cash register and above Johnson's head read, "No balances carried over after June 1, 1909." Merchants needed to mind their books, as it was common for customers to charge their groceries to an account. In 1915, the Ersfeld family took over the Johnson & Reioux Meat Market, which would last for three generations and close in 2006. (Courtesy of LoraLee Briley.)

It is clearly wintertime in this 1908 photograph, and a horse is seen in the background wearing a blanket. Nothing remains today of old South Lake Street. Most of what is seen here was gone by the 1960s. The Forest Lake Roller Mills structure was relocated across the street and eventually scrapped for lumber, which was used in the old E.J. Houle Grain Elevator building. (Courtesy of the Forest Lake Historical Society.)

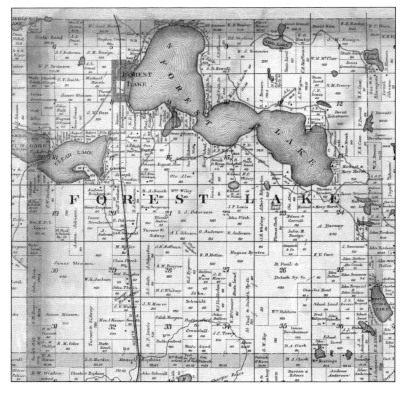

This 1887 map published by C.M. Foote & Co. is part of a larger map that encompasses Ramsey and Washington Counties along with parts of neighboring counties. It is the earliest plat map of Forest Lake with owners' names known to exist and offers a wealth of information about the town's early days. (Courtesy of the Library of Congress.)

The biggest industry near Forest Lake at the turn of the 20th century was the American Grass Twine Company. Based out of St. Paul, the raw material was harvested from the peat bogs in the upper Midwest, including nearby Columbus. It was useless in just about every way but somehow found an unexpected niche in producing a range of household goods, from carpets to music stands—260 products in all by 1903. A network of harvest camps was set up that ran from July to the first frost gathering wire grass and binding it into large bales for shipment to St. Paul. In 1908, American Grass Twine became the Crex Carpet Company, which focused solely on the production of carpets. They were cheap to make and could be dyed any color. Soon, Crex was employing hundreds of factory workers, who operated mechanized looms to produce the carpets. However, Crex would later run into competition with Japan's inferior but cheaper grass rugs and declared bankruptcy in 1935. (Courtesy of Ken DuFresne.)

Art Bergerson manages the horse while Gust Johnson mows. To everyone else, the Fourth of July signaled the celebration of Independence Day. To the workers of wire grass camps, it signaled the beginning of harvesting season. As the wire grass turned from green to hazy blue, it was ready and the process began. (Courtesy of Ken DuFresne.)

Carl Engquist was the foreman of the gleaner crew in 1909. The mechanical sheaf binder, or gleaner, seen here would gather the recently cut wire grass and bind it together into bundles to be taken to sheds for storage. Once enough wire grass was bundled, it would be pressed and baled for the trip into Forest Lake. (Courtesy of Ken DuFresne.)

The phrase "needle in a haystack" could just as well be applied to a mountain of harvested wire grass. Crew members demonstrate to the camera just how much work was done and the meal they will enjoy for their efforts. In the back right, a harvesting crew member demonstrates how bog shoes were applied to the horses. This mound of wire grass would be processed into many bales weighing approximately 200 pounds each. It would then make its way by horse and wagon into Forest Lake, where it would be stored in the large Crex warehouse by the railroad depot to await its final journey by train to St. Paul. There were three wire grass camps in the area. Camp One was west of Wyoming, with Camp Two just south of it. Camp Three was west of Forest Lake. Camp Three Road in Columbus is the only remaining evidence of a booming industry that swept through the area. (Courtesy of Ken DuFresne.)

The most important man in the camp was the cook (or "cookie"). Depending on how well he did, the workers would either stick around or leave for another camp that had better cuisine. Of course, the meals were all the same: salt pork and potatoes with lots of pastries and coffee. Cook Frank Shotl is seen here with his utensils. (Courtesy of Ken DuFresne.)

The wire grass harvesters ate and slept at the camps. The work was 10 hours per day, seven days a week. It was literally backbreaking work. No drinking or gambling was allowed, and only English was permitted. After a day of brutal, hot weather and tiring work, the workers climbed into their tents and bunkhouses, the lice being their only companions. (Courtesy of Ken DuFresne.)

Three

CHURCHES AND SCHOOLS

This was Forest Lake's first school, built in 1874. One teacher taught all grades until the 1894–1895 term, when an addition was built onto the school. At one point, teacher and principal R.F. Swails had 60 pupils in his class. This led to the opening of a new school in 1909. The original school was turned into a town hall and destroyed by fire in 1913. (Courtesy of Washington County Historical Society.)

Forest Lake's first photographer, S.B. Howell, took this photograph in 1888. A Mr. Gross is the teacher standing at left. The last names of these students represent some of the earliest settlers in Forest Lake: Simmons, Stipe, Rahm, Peoples, and York. J.L. Simmons is standing at top right; his future wife is to his right. (Courtesy of LoraLee Briley.)

The Alm School, District No. 67, was built in 1886 near the southwest corner of Highway 97 and Harrow Avenue North. It served first through seventh grades. Students sat at double desks and warmed their lunches around the wood-burning stove. The boys took turns bringing in wood from the woodpile. Teacher Sena Nelson is seen here with her 42 pupils in 1904. (Courtesy of Faith Lutheran Church.)

This school is the only reminder of the town of Garen that once stood at the crossroads of Highway 61 and 190th Street North. The Northern Pacific Railway agreed to create a switch line so farmers could load their cattle into boxcars to be shipped to South St. Paul. A boxcar was even used as the train station, with a wooden platform built around it. The stop was named Garen, after the families who lived there. The tiny town consisted of a general store, tavern, school, and some cattle pens. Although not a scheduled stop, passengers could flag down the train if they wanted a ride. In approximately 1934, children were bused to school in Forest Lake, and the Garen schoolhouse became vacant. In 1951, the schoolhouse was destroyed by fire and the town of Garen ceased to exist. (Courtesy of Cheryl Johnson.)

Work began on a new school in the spring of 1909 at a cost of about $20,000. The plans called for a 62-by-72-square-foot building "of pressed brick and cut stone, hard wall plaster . . . containing eight school rooms, classrooms and assembly hall." Although ready for use that fall, only the first few floors were complete due to funding. The rest of the school was completed the following year. Forest Lake was now able to serve all grades up to 12 and graduated its first class in 1912, consisting solely of George Simmons. It was near the southwest corner of SW Third Street and Second Avenue SW—historically, Ash Street and Tenth Avenue. During the first year, George Bakalyar was principal; Secundilla McVey taught eighth grade; Edna Bailey, fifth, sixth, and seventh grades; Hazel Lord, third and fourth grades; and Maurine Clark, first and second grades. After the 1920 school was built, this building served as a grade school until it was condemned in 1977. (Courtesy of the Forest Lake Historical Society.)

Reynold Erickson (left) and Al Lellman pause for a quick photograph in the boiler room of the 1909 school building. Erickson invented the folding cafeteria table in 1948 and assisted with the design of the current high school. Lellman was known by students for being a grandfather-like figure always willing to lend an ear. (Courtesy of the Forest Lake Historical Society.)

The second graduating class in Forest Lake produced a state representative in the Minnesota legislature. Rollin G. Johnson (second row, left) also served as a commissioner on the Minnesota Railroad and Warehouse Commission. From left to right are (first row) Principal Monica McElroy, Amelia Evens, Etta Simmons, Esther Nelson, and Supt. Frank J. Oliver; (second row) Johnson and Roy Sawyer. (Courtesy of the Forest Lake Historical Society.)

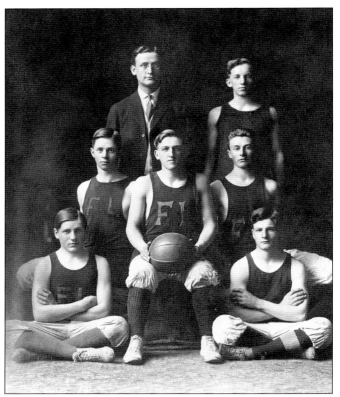

The Forest Lake basketball team was likely the first team sport at the high school. This photograph is from the 1912–1913 season. Supt. Frank J. Oliver (third row, left) wore many hats in the early days. From left to right are (first row) Jim Vail and Dick Simmons; (second row) Howard Struble, Rollin G. Johnson, and Roy Sawyer; (third row) Oliver and Harold Swanson. (Courtesy of the Forest Lake Historical Society.)

This photograph taken in 1920 shows the construction of the new high school just south of the 1909 school. The total cost of the addition was $120,000. A passageway was added between the two schools. More changes would be added over the years, with the most recent demolition and upgrades occurring in 2021. (Courtesy of the Forest Lake Historical Society.)

The new 1909 school was able to serve the education needs of Forest Lake for just 11 short years. When the 1920 school was built, it became the first dedicated high school, and the old school was designated for grades one through eight. A one-level public library was also built in between. Inside the school, a large, all-purpose gymnasium on the first floor could accommodate more sports. A balcony above allowed students to watch the games below. On one side was a stage for performing plays and operettas. The 1920 school was able to meet the needs of Forest Lake students for nearly 30 years. The first superintendent of the school was W.R. Fieldhouse, followed by J.W. Perry in 1925 and E.S. Doty in 1928. B.C. Kuefler served as superintendent for over 20 years. (Courtesy of the Forest Lake Historical Society.)

The is the earliest photograph of a girls' basketball team that has been found. The 1921–1922 team is pictured with their coach in the gymnasium of the new 1920 high school. At the time, girls were encouraged to play more ladylike sports such as swimming, tennis, and golf. (Courtesy of Brian Tolzmann.)

This staged photograph of a tip-off was taken by local photographer Nick Mitsoff. Frances Grieman is on the right, with both women assuming the proper stance. In the early 1930s, the girls' basketball team was discontinued for a time. (Courtesy of Diane Knutson.)

Since the baseball season ran contrary to the yearbook season, baseball did not get much publicity. Basketball and football reigned supreme, and thus, photographs like this are a rarity. It was likely taken in the 1920s. The only person identified is teacher and coach Carl C. Perry. (Courtesy of Diane Knutson.)

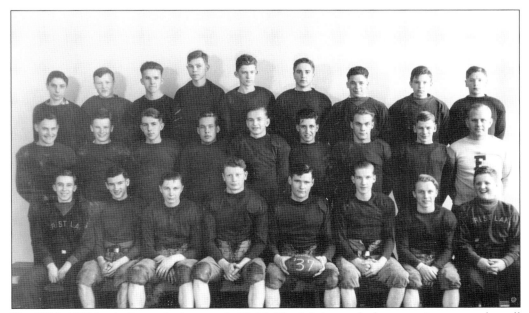

The 1936–1937 football team had a record of 2-4-1. The 0-0 tie was the homecoming game, when all the businesses in town were closed for the afternoon. The following year's record, albeit incomplete, was 1-1-1. As with any sports team, the Forest Lake football team endured a long slump. No one has been identified in this photograph. (Courtesy of the Gary Moen family.)

The 1931 Junior-Senior Banquet was held at the Forest Lake Town and Country Club. Built in 1927 at the cost of $100,000, the club was billed as having a first-class café and entertainment. It had a large stone fireplace, beautiful hardwood floors, and an elegant white staircase that led upstairs to six rooms for out-of-town guests. Its enclosed glass porch looked out over the lake and was also an area to watch golfers coming in from the ninth hole. Barney Carlson was the new golf pro, a former pro at Phalen Golf Course in St. Paul. The clubhouse held many banquets, parties, and dances over the years. It was just south of the cul-de-sac on Harrow Avenue North near Second Lake. When the golf course was redesigned in the early 1980s to accommodate new townhomes, the old country club was not in the plans. It was demolished in 1984. (Courtesy of Diane Knutson.)

The junior class of Forest Lake High School presented the play *The Tin Hero* in 1936. Pictured are, from left to right, (first row) Marion Landgraver, Lucille Fuglie, Carole Engquist, and Genevieve Moen; (second row) two unidentified; (third row) Anthony Bronczyk, Ruth Taylor, Lawrence Frenning, Pearl Novak, Esther ?, Cy ?, Doris Cyr, Clint Fladland, Anna Rainer, and Beatrice Diekman. (Courtesy of the Gary Moen family.)

This is the Little German Band from the 1937–1938 school year. From left to right are Daniel Sundberg, Anita Waller, Katherine Tolzmann, Harriet Rieck, Alan Larson, Charles Dupre, and band director Milo Phelps. Phelps went on to direct the Superior (Wisconsin) Shipyard Band during World War II. (Courtesy of the Gary Moen family.)

Pictured here are, from left to right, high school principal Kenneth Von Wald, elementary principal Grace Johnstone, assistant high school principal Floyd Cohoes, and superintendent B.C. Kuefler. Kuefler came to Forest Lake in 1930 and was superintendent for 20 years. Cohoes served a longer term as principal, from 1949 to 1972. (Courtesy of Corbett Johnson.)

World War II propaganda was everywhere, including the schools. The 1944–1945 yearbook was dedicated to "The Cause," with an entire military theme. A poster on the wall reads, "Stamp out the Axis with bonds and stamps." Here, Ray Hanson (left) and Floyd Cohoes look over the shoulders of Solveig Hammond (center) and two other women. (Courtesy of Corbett Johnson.)

PAVED, NOW!

PUBLIC SCHOOL BUILDINGS — FOREST LAKE — MINN — A-7602

By 1953, an addition was needed once again to accommodate the needs of the growing student population. In 1948, a wing had been added to the north side of the 1909 grade school, and in 1951, the rural schools were consolidated into one school district. At a cost of over half a million dollars, this new structure added a large gymnasium, multiple classrooms, and a basement with lockers and showers. To keep the latter areas warm during the winter, radiant copper coils embedded in the concrete and supplemental hot air ducts were used—a modern improvement for the day. The old gymnasium in the 1920 building was converted into a combination cafeteria/study hall. The dedication ceremony was held with a guest speaker, Dean Schweickhard, commissioner of education. His topic was "Building for Tomorrow." (Courtesy of the Forest Lake Historical Society.)

Chili burgers, chicken noodle soup, and mashed potatoes with hamburger gravy were just some of the favorite meals prepared by these school cooks. From left to right are Florence Collins, Linda Rosckes, Inga Schmidt, Peg Ekdahl, Agnes Patrin, Myrtle Garen, and Grace Anderson. (Courtesy of Corliss Vadner.)

Grace (Stephenson) Coy poses for the camera in this undated photograph. She was secretary to superintendent B.C. Kuefler. In addition to doing most of Kuefler's typing, her other tasks included bookkeeping, filing, answering phone calls, and marking report cards. She was also the head of the statewide school secretaries association. Outside of her school life, she enjoyed cooking and photography. (Courtesy of Sue Ruggles-Coy.)

A school bus picks up children in this 1920s photograph. It appears to be a mash-up between a Model T and a trolley car. The school district had 10 buses by this time. This particular model may have been built by Wayne Works, an automotive company in Indiana that was one of the top producers of school transport in the country. (Courtesy of the Gary Moen family.)

This more familiar and modern view of a school bus is from about 1972 and includes all the bus drivers for the school district. The bus garage on the north end of town now had a fleet of buses that could accommodate four times as many students. (Courtesy of Corliss Vadner.)

The Swedish Evangelical Lutheran Church sat on the northwest corner of Second Avenue NW and Northwest Third Street. The congregation formed in 1888 and met at the Alm Schoolhouse for the first five years. In 1892, their church building was completed. This photograph was taken in 1904. (Courtesy of Faith Lutheran Church.)

The church sanctuary in 1920 was simple and unadorned for its time. The altar appears to be against the wall, with the celebrant's back toward the congregation during preparation of Communion. An altar rail encloses the space, and a single, perpetual light hangs above. Pastor Arthur Knock is shown in the inset. (Courtesy of Faith Lutheran Church.)

On October 13, 1960, a fire broke out at the Lutheran church around 8:30 in the morning. As Dennis Johnson was biking to school, he saw smoke coming out of the church and notified Pastor Frank Johnson. The fire was quickly called in. By the time the firefighters arrived, the blaze was already spreading up the walls into the belfry. Neighboring fire departments gave assistance while parishioners ran in to save precious items from the fire. Onlookers could not help but stare in disbelief, some grabbing cameras to document the moment for posterity. Many recall the heartbreaking thud of the bell hitting the floor. This photograph was taken just as the gold-painted cross fell. The cause of the fire was later determined to be electrical. A meeting had been held that spring to discuss future building plans, which also included a decision to replace the outdated wiring in the current church. (Courtesy of Faith Lutheran Church.)

Parishioner Bob Severson inspects the work on the new Lutheran church sanctuary, now relocated to 886 North Shore Drive in Forest Lake. Although a tragedy, the fire was a blessing in disguise, as the congregation was growing far too quickly and the on-street parking at the prior location was becoming too congested for the area. (Courtesy of Faith Lutheran Church.)

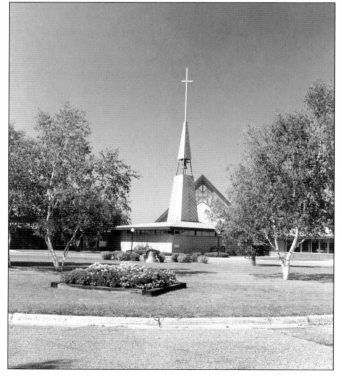

The new Faith Lutheran Church had its first Sunday service on August 11, 1963. It was the first time in nearly three years that the congregants could gather in their own building. Following the service, the cornerstone was laid. The new building was also completed in time for the 75th anniversary. (Courtesy of Faith Lutheran Church.)

St. Peter's Catholic Church was built in June 1905 in response to the growing congregation in neighboring Wyoming. J.W. Houle donated two lots on the northwest corner of Broadway Avenue and Northwest Fifth Street, and the foundation was laid in 1904. Meanwhile, the parishioners gathered in the Modern Woodmen's Hall over Young's Hardware Store until the church was completed. (Courtesy of the Forest Lake Historical Society.)

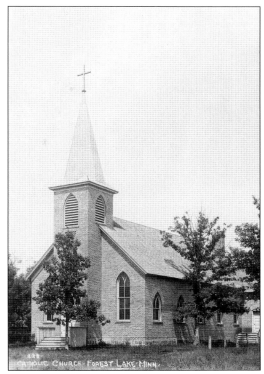

Much like the Swedish Lutheran Church, St. Peter's was growing and needed more room to spread out. It relocated to a piece of farmland just south of Beltz Park and was rebuilt in 1961. A convent was also built nearby that housed the Sisters of Notre Dame. They became the teachers for the new school that adjoined the church. (Courtesy of St. Peter's Church.)

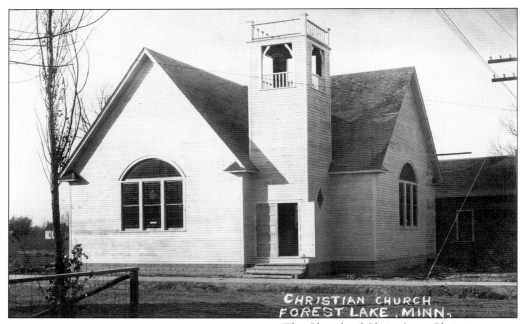

CHRISTIAN CHURCH
FOREST LAKE, MINN,

The Church of Christ (now Christian Church) has been in the same spot for the past 113 years; a distinction no other local church has. Located on the southwest corner of Broadway Avenue and Fourth Street SW, the church's dedication took place in 1910 with 32 charter members. The first minister was Richard Dobson. The church was destroyed by fire in 1942 and rebuilt in 1952. (Courtesy of the Forest Lake Historical Society.)

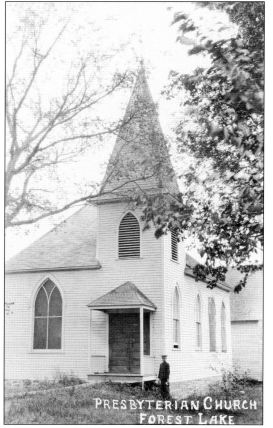

PRESBYTERIAN CHURCH
FOREST LAKE

The Presbyterian church was constructed in 1904 near the northeast corner of Lake Avenue North and Northeast Second Avenue. It was built by John Marsh, the lowest bidder at $2,895. Part of several mission churches, its name was Faith, with sister churches Hope and Charity in neighboring Columbus and Oneka (now Hugo), respectively. (Courtesy of the Forest Lake Historical Society.)

Four

A GROWING CITY

J.L. Simmons stands near the doorway of his dry goods store on North Lake Street in 1909. This building is said to have been built in 1891, making it the oldest commercial structure in town still standing today. It sold just about everything in its day, including fabric, glassware, pots, pans, boots, shoes, clothing, and more. Today, it is the home of Rolseth Drug. (Courtesy of LoraLee Briley.)

It is a busy day at the Forest Lake Cooperative Creamery. Farmers would load up their cream cans in the back of the wagon and head to town. Cream-buying days were usually three days a week, which allowed farmers to take care of errands and visit with friends while in town. It is not known when the creamery was formed, as the initial document was not dated. It reads, in part, "We, the undersigned citizens of Washington, Chisago and Anoka Counties, state of Minnesota, do hereby agree to form ourselves into an association to be known by the name of the Forest Lake Cooperative Creamery Association, and we agree to borrow the sum of three-thousand dollars or less, to put up a building and equip it with the necessary machinery." At the bottom of the document, each farmer signed his name with the number of cows he owned. A.W. Johnson had the most, with 13. The original building burned down in 1930 and was replaced with a modern brick structure. (Courtesy of Diane Knutson.)

Ersfeld's Meat Market ran for 91 years in Forest Lake in the same building constructed around 1900. The day started at 5:00 a.m. and often continued until 8:00 p.m. Bacon, hams, and smoked bologna were readily available. A walk-in cooler needed 15 cakes of ice weighing 400 pounds each to keep food cool. Here, Henry Ersfeld (left) and business partner John Murray stand poised and ready for the next customer. (Courtesy of Bert and Elsie Vogel.)

The Forest Lake chapter of Royal Neighbors was started in the early 1900s by a group of women who wanted to work for the common good of the town. The organization also provided insurance to women nationally, much like the Modern Woodmen of America did at the time. This photograph shows a group that attended a Royal Neighbors picnic in 1910. (Courtesy of the Forest Lake Historical Society.)

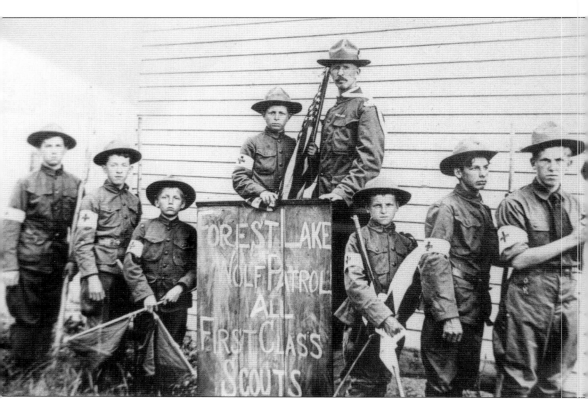

The Boy Scouts of America was modeled on the Boy Scouts Association established in Britain in 1908. When the BSA was incorporated on February 8, 1910, several other scouting organizations followed suit, including one started by William Randolph Hearst. When the BSA National Office opened in June, the applications started to come in. By fall, there were 2,500 leader applications from 44 states. Rev. G.R. Gilruth Fisher, pastor of the Forest Lake Presbyterian Church, was responsible for organizing the Scout unit. Though the claim has not yet been substantiated by original documentation, it is said that Fisher formed the first troop in Minnesota in July 1910. The Wolf Patrol is seen here in 1911 after winning their Red Cross badges. From left to right are Howard Carter, Livingstone "Levi" Fisher, Harry Smalley, Stanley Struble, Reverend Fisher, Gilmore Fisher, Arley Walker, and Ernest Bacheller. (Courtesy of Washington County Historical Society.)

The Forest Lake State Bank was started by Orlando and Wayne Struble in 1903. It spent the first year in this structure, then moved a few buildings south the following year. Wayne Struble, the first cashier, stands in front. The kerosene lamps in town, like the one seen here in the foreground, were lit nightly and extinguished each morning by the night marshal. (Courtesy of Washington County Historical Society.)

Inside the bank, customer Nellie Banta poses for a photograph before conducting business. At the center window is Orlando Struble, and the cashier at right is Harlan W. Swanson. A sign to the left of the window reads, "Honor thy Father and Mother, but not the stranger's checks." (Courtesy of Washington County Historical Society.)

Although mail delivery had existed for many years, Forest Lake did not have a permanent post office building until around 1910. It was located at present-day 115 North Lake Street. The brick facade has since been changed and the side windows covered. This photograph, dated 1911, shows a vacant spot at left where the first theater building would soon be constructed. (Courtesy of Washington County Historical Society.)

Inside the post office, everyone is posing for the photographer. At right, a man fills out a deposit slip while the person to his left drops off a package. Note how small the service windows were. A calendar on the wall dates this photograph to April 1916, and a sign in the foreground warns customers not to spit on the floor, lest it spread disease. (Courtesy of Washington County Historical Society.)

PARK SCENE, FOREST LAKE, MINN. 328

The rectangular property owned by the railroad on which the train depot sat was rather unsightly for many years, having served no other purpose but to get people from here to there. In 1893, the village council petitioned the Northern Pacific Railway to allow the creation of a park for the citizens to enjoy. After the ground was leveled, a fence was installed around the perimeter and trees planted. Benches were installed throughout the park. Eventually, a bandstand was built as well as a few tennis courts. The Forest Lake Garden Club planted many attractive flowers around the park. This area was enjoyed by citizens for many years until the commercial district began to close in. After further expansion, the trees were felled, and the bandstand was moved to the new lakeside park. (Courtesy of the Forest Lake Historical Society.)

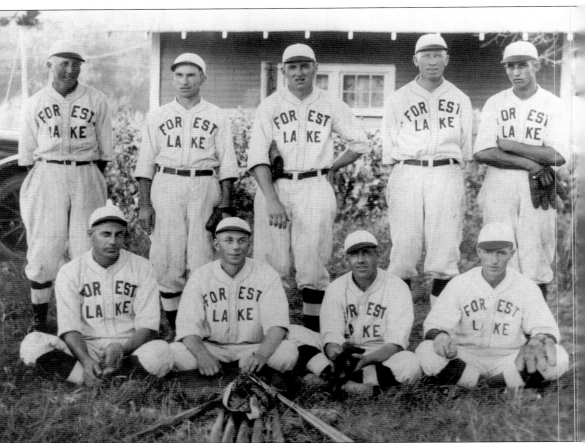

Amateur baseball enjoyed its peak popularity across the country from the 1920s through the 1950s. However, baseball had been a part of Forest Lake for many years prior. The first known documented game was on July 1, 1894, against Taylors Falls, where the latter won 14-6 at a home game. Teams were called "the nines" for the obvious reason of having nine players on the field. Many business owners like Tony Valenty, Frank Walker, and Dr. Poirier were part of the early teams. Pictured here is the Forest Lake baseball team of 1923. From left to right are (first row) E.J. Houle, second base; Fritz Stille, catcher; Dewey Spickler, third base; and Orlo Tracy, pitcher; (second row) Oscar Peterson, shortstop; Tony Patrin, right field; Norman "Sandy" Gowan, left field; Milton Peterson, first base; and Kenneth Poirier, center field. Kenneth was a son of Dr. Poirier. (Courtesy of Corliss Vadner.)

In 1916, L.P. Melbostad continued the grocery store tradition by purchasing the building previously owned by A.W. Johnson. By this time, fruits and vegetables were replacing farm implements and other nonperishable goods as customers began to recognize the value in a diverse selection of food. At left, a delivery truck waits for its next order. (Courtesy of Sue Erickson.)

Inside L.P. Melbostad's grocery store, an assortment of goods is on display. However, grocery shopping was mostly done over the phone. Telephone orders came in the morning, and deliveries were made in the afternoon. The summer months kept the drivers busy, especially when driving around the large lake. (Courtesy of Sue Erickson.)

Brothers Frank (center) and Homer (second from right) Wilson came from Illinois in search of opportunity and settled in Forest Lake to take over a recently established newspaper—the *Forest Lake Advertiser*. In this photograph, their mother (left) has come out to visit her prosperous sons. A cousin, Fred Wilson, stands second from left. Wildie Heil, typesetter, is at right. (Courtesy of Forest Lake Historical Society.)

This is the inside of the *Forest Lake Advertiser* in June 1909. The exact location has not yet been determined. The precursor to the *Advertiser* was the *Enterprise*, which was started in 1903 by Howard Folsom and printed in a corner of the E.J. Houle potato warehouse. Typesetter Wildie Heil stands at center. The others are unidentified. (Courtesy of LoraLee Briley.)

Tobacconist Tony Valenty stands behind the fully stocked counter of cigars, cigarettes, tobacco, and snuff. He carried a vast number of cigars, even ones made by a local judge, H.E. Driese. At the very left, enough pipes appear to be available for every man in town. Valenty also sold penny candy and ice cream and was adept at repairing watches and clocks. He even did engraving on jewelry. Billiard tables were located in the back, and a barbershop was near the entrance. Barber John Grieman and his brother Joe first set up their business at Valenty's. Patrons (exclusively men) found Valenty's parlor a welcome break from the monotony of the day. After Prohibition was repealed, Tony Valenty and his brother George were issued a liquor license. George ran the bar in a separate room next to the pool hall. In this photograph, Fred Owens (center) and Jack Altenberger stop in to visit. (Courtesy of Forest Lake Historical Society.)

The newly constructed Carpenter Oil building sat on the northwest corner of Broadway Avenue and Lake Street, just near the railroad tracks. Tragically, the prior building went up in a spectacular blaze on the afternoon of June 30, 1923. According to firefighter Rube Engler, gas was being unloaded from the railroad tank cars into the storage tanks by a pumper motor in a small building. Across the street, business owner Ben Peterson noticed gas running out of the tank and ran to tell Frank Carpenter. Just then, a spark from the motor ignited the overflowing gas. As Carpenter reached to switch off the motor, approximately 50,000 gallons of gasoline ignited. Nearby residents heard the explosion and went to find out what was going on. Carpenter was badly burned and taken to St. John's Hospital in St. Paul. Peterson suffered burns to his hands and face, and firefighter Harold Brown was injured carrying automobile accessories from the garage. Carpenter died the following day from his injuries. (Courtesy of the Forest Lake Historical Society.)

The Commercial Hotel stands on the north end of town—a symbol of progress and strength with its brick exterior and concrete entryway. It replaced the short-lived Hotel Vexio, thought to be the original business built there around 1911. Of all the hotels in Forest Lake's past, the Commercial is the only one remaining. (Courtesy of Sue Erickson.)

Concrete block rapidly replaces the old stone foundations. The amount of lake homes increases as farmers with large lake lots begin to sell off smaller lots. Concrete contractor Frank Stipe is seen here making sure every block is lined up straight. (Courtesy of Diane Knutson.)

This is the residence of druggist Richard F. Petersen at present-day 179 South Shore Drive. Born in Wabasha, Minnesota, he moved to Forest Lake and, along with business partner Hugh Smith, bought the former Diekman's Pharmacy in 1935. Petersen was in business until 1961, when he sold to his successor, Tom Rolseth. (Courtesy of the Forest Lake Historical Society.)

Photographs of the main street taken before 1926 were often labeled "B.C." (before cement). The change from dirt to pavement was a catharsis for many residents who endured years of choking dust and stubborn mud. This photograph taken around 1927 shows a dapper Lake Street view. (Courtesy of the Forest Lake Historical Society.)

Forest Lake has had several village/city halls over the years. When the township was established in 1874, a town hall did not exist. Village leaders would meet at the train depot, schoolhouse, and even Michael Marsh's residence for several years until one could be built. In 1887, Olaus Anderson was paid $75 to erect the first town hall to exact specifications. It is not known if another town hall existed in between the first one and the one pictured here. This building was constructed in the fall of 1939 and dedicated in 1940. A library was added the following year. It would serve the needs of Forest Lake for over 35 years until the decision was made to construct a new city hall/ civic center/library complex on the same spot, which opened in 1978. (Courtesy of the Forest Lake Historical Society.)

Country Club Golf Course - Forest Lake Minn A-7613

This view of the Forest Lake Country Club looks more like a manicured farm than a golf course. Photographed from the corner of Highway 97 and Harrow Avenue North, the clubhouse was situated within the distant grove of trees, just near the lake. Ray Van Syoc and A.B. Johnson purchased the land in 1926. The fairways were initially graded and seeded. The greens were constructed the following spring and originally made of sand, later to be replaced by grass. The course opened in May 1927 and was featured prominently in the American Legion's Fourth of July program. It was a public course for the first two years, but according to a newspaper article in 1929, it was changed to private and referred to as the Lakeside Country Club, with a membership of 350. In 1935, the course was purchased by Ed and Hazel Langan. Starting in 1944 during World War II, the course was turned into a turkey farm and then back to a golf course a few years later. (Courtesy of the Forest Lake Historical Society.)

Harold and Ann Moen share a moment near the beach at the Forest Lake Country Club. The couple behind them are unidentified. Unlike today, the golf course had 500 feet of lakeshore property abutting Second Lake. The enclosed porch of the clubhouse seen here provided magnificent views. The person holding the camera would likely be standing near the cul-de-sac on Harrow Avenue North. (Courtesy of the Gary Moen family.)

Looking north, just south of town, Highway 61 was much quieter. The tree-lined street was mostly residential, with lake cabins and summer homes to the right. A small service station appears in the distance, and the arm of an old-fashioned streetlamp reaches over the road. Today, this view would be completely unrecognizable. (Courtesy of the Forest Lake Historical Society.)

Nickolas Mitsoff was born in 1891 in Bulgaria and settled in Minneapolis. He worked as a laborer in a steel factory before getting a job at the Orpheum Photo Studio. He started his photography business and moved to Forest Lake in 1922. He was the town photographer for many years until his death in 1950. (Courtesy of the Mitsoff family.)

This photograph was taken inside Nick Mitsoff's studio. A variety of made-to-order picture frames line the shelf above. This group of unidentified high school students dropped in to have photographs taken. Clara (Skoglund) Hehner was Mitsoff's assistant and rescued many discarded photographs, including this one. (Courtesy of Diane Knutson.)

Dr. George Ruggles opened his first clinic office in 1932 in downtown Forest Lake. Drafted into service during World War II in 1942, he set his sights on bigger things when he returned home in 1945. The following year, he purchased an old farmhouse and turned it into Forest Lake's first hospital. It opened in 1948 and continued to serve the community until its closing in 1962. (Courtesy of the Ruggles family.)

This was the first hospital in Forest Lake, at present-day 107 South Shore Drive. At the turn of the 20th century, it was a dairy farm owned by a wealthy family from St. Paul. It was then sold in 1911 to Charles Beard, a real estate salesman. When he died in 1945, it gave Dr. Ruggles the opportunity to purchase the property in 1946. (Courtesy of Sue Ruggles-Coy.)

The story of Hugh Hamilton Hehner is one of both success and tragedy. Born in 1901 to parents Samuel and Lillian, Hehner grew up in a farming family but had bigger aspirations. At the time, the study of chiropractic was generally not seen as alternative medicine but as a "bastardized version of osteopathy." Still, Hehner saw a future in its practice and attended the Palmer School of Chiropractic in Davenport, Iowa—the first school of its kind in the world. He graduated in 1924 and obtained his license in March 1925. Returning to his hometown of Forest Lake, he opened his practice that April 1 in the Park Café Building on Lake Street South. His list of patients grew quickly. A mere six months later, Hehner contracted typhoid and died at the home of his parents; an unfortunate end to a promising life and career. (Courtesy of the Forest Lake Historical Society.)

Five

THE LAKE

In this 1906 photograph, a man attempts to row from Berggren's Landing on First Lake, just north of present-day Sunshine Court. Victor and Hulda Berggren ran the Forest Home Hotel at the time, which operated from 1879 to 1913. The original proprietors are unknown. The sender of this postcard assures the recipient that the beach has been cleaned up and is now "fine for bathing." (Courtesy of the Forest Lake Historical Society.)

Pleasure-seekers are enjoying some time out on First Lake. Rowboats were readily available at the Forest Lake landing or nearby resorts. For an extra fee, a guide was available to reveal the best fishing spots or to show customers around the lake. (Courtesy of the Forest Lake Historical Society.)

Although not identified by location, brothers Hill and Grant Brown are pictured here with a group of friends and family for a 15-day camping trip in Forest Lake. The same group appears in the previous photograph. It is difficult to imagine such a lengthy trip in the outdoors, especially in the middle of July. Weather records for those two weeks indicate several days in the 90s, with scant precipitation. (Courtesy of the Forest Lake Historical Society.)

A duck blind sits on a sandy point on Third Lake surrounded by reeds. A perfect spot for hunting, it was aptly named "Duck Pass." Simmons Point, between Second and Third Lakes, was another popular hunting spot. This photograph dates to around 1908. (Courtesy of the Forest Lake Historical Society.)

Simmons Point looked much different nearly 100 years ago. Named after one of its owners, J.L. Simmons, it was a popular spot for swimming, hunting, and the occasional wiener roast. It is still a popular swimming area today. Ownership records go back to 1855, when it was first owned by Richard P. Frederick. (Courtesy of the Forest Lake Historical Society.)

This is one of the oldest known photographs of the point, taken around 1916. Here, it is more of a sandbar than a point of land lined with trees. The point itself is unique, as it sits within Sections 10, 11, 14, and 15. Therefore, this tiny peninsula was platted as four parcels of land. (Courtesy of the Forest Lake Historical Society.)

This dirt road was essentially the eastern terminus of Broadway Avenue, near the present-day roundabout next to the park. The boat landing was to the right, Boehm's boat livery and bait shop was at center, and the open-air Pavilion was at left. This photograph dates to the 1920s. (Courtesy of Washington County Historical Society.)

BOAT LANDING, FOREST LAKE, MINN.

The boat landing seen here in the foreground around 1909 belonged to an unidentified competitor of John Boehm, whose landing is seen in the background. Boehm convinced his competitor to merge with him into one large boat livery and soon after bought him out. Boehm started his business in 1901, purchasing the landing from Mitt Simmons. He paid the village a rental fee of $100 yearly and kept up the maintenance at the park. He would meet train passengers and take boat reservations right at the depot. Launches were also offered at $1.50 to go to Third Lake, $1 to Second Lake, and 50¢ anywhere on First Lake. He also supplied boaters with bait if they needed it. On busy days, his daughters would come to help, often bringing him meals when needed. Boehm sold his business in 1948. (Courtesy of the Forest Lake Historical Society.)

Unlike the grand lake homes that are seen today, these humble cabins lined the shores of Forest Lake for over a century. Very little accoutrements were necessary in those days. Here, an overturned canoe rests near the beach after a day's outing, and an enclosed porch provided cool lake breezes on hot summer nights. This photograph dates from around 1920. (Courtesy of the Forest Lake Historical Society.)

The Sunshine Camp and the West Side Social and Outing Club both converge on the camping grounds in this unknown location. Not much is known of either club; however, the Sunshine Camp may have been an extension of the International Sunshine Society that founded the Mary Davis Sunshine Lodge. (Courtesy of the Forest Lake Historical Society.)

The original bathing beach was built and operated from the early 1920s until the late 1930s. The bathhouse was built in a T shape, with wings on either side for men and women to change into their suits. Numbered tin boxes for clothes storage were rented for 4¢. Bathing suits and towels could also be rented. Drinks, candy, and ice cream were sold at the counter, with the favorite item being frozen Snickers bars. Big willow trees provided plenty of shade for picnics. The main attraction was a large wooden toboggan slide. It was high and steep and went right into the water. In 1937, Ran Lake and his wife, Irene, bought the bathing beach and developed it into a cabin court. It operated as a resort for the next 40 years and was the last one on Forest Lake. (Courtesy of the Forest Lake Historical Society.)

The open-air dance pavilion was near the bathing beach and was a popular destination for locals. The music could be heard all over the lake, with local musicians providing some of the music. A popular band was Peps Snuggle Pups, with Bud Pepin playing saxophone, Lou Heim on piano, and Loren Alshouse on drums. (Courtesy of the Forest Lake Historical Society.)

This photograph taken around 1907 is thought to be of children from the newly established Mary Davis Sunshine Lodge. It was taken on the west end of First Lake, just north of Boehm's Landing. At the time, the lodge was downtown in the spot where the Lighthouse Lofts building sits. Part of the lodge included a large lake lot for children to swim. (Courtesy of the Forest Lake Historical Society.)

VILLAUME'S LANDING. FOREST LAKE. MINN.

This is Villaume's Landing in the 1910s. Eugene Villaume ran a successful box and lumber company out of St. Paul and had a large summer home in Forest Lake on the corner of Northeast Fourth Avenue and North Shore Drive. The house still stands today. It was originally a sanitarium at the turn of the 20th century, which only lasted about a year. (Courtesy of the Forest Lake Historical Society.)

It is difficult enough to get a few people to face the camera for a photograph, let alone hundreds. The employees of the Northern Pacific Railway General Office gathered in Forest Lake on July 24, 1915, for a company picnic. The boat landing near downtown was a popular destination for

Northern Pacific Railway
General Office Employees Picnic,
Forest Lake, Minn. July 24, – 1915.

businesses to bring their employees for a day of relaxation and entertainment. (Courtesy of the Minnesota Historical Society.)

The Lakeside Cabin Court was about a block south of Broadway Avenue and consisted of 16 cabins along 100 feet of lakeshore. It was first owned by Frank Hoffman and Frank Wold in the late 1930s and later sold to partners E.F. and Ginny Lehmann and Art and Fran Palmer. The price for cabins was $3.50 for singles and $5.50 for doubles. Laundry was especially time-consuming before dryers were in use, and sometimes took all day. One famous guest was the flamboyant wrestler Gorgeous George. He arrived in his purple Cadillac and sprayed perfume wherever he went. He had his hair cut by Gladys Boreen in her beauty shop in the Herzberg building. George wore gold-plated bobby pins in his hair and would pass them out to people, calling them "Georgie Pins." (Courtesy of the Forest Lake Historical Society.)

Ran Lake and his wife, Irene, developed the former bathing beach site into a 12-unit cabin court in 1937. Small, white cabins with flower boxes encircled an inner area with tables and chairs. A large, sandy beach and a dock with boat rentals were at hand for guests who wanted to enjoy all the lake had to offer. (Courtesy of the Forest Lake Historical Society.)

This is Ran's Cabins as seen from the lake. A sign warns noncustomers to keep off the dock. It would later be called Nelson's Cabins and was eventually demolished in 1978 for new lakeshore condominiums. It was the last surviving resort on Forest Lake. (Courtesy of the Forest Lake Historical Society.)

Bowman's Resort was on North Shore Drive at the source of the Sunrise River. It was owned by Ray Bowman, who had several log cabins for rent with sweeping views of First Lake. There was even a railroad car on the property that was rented out. In 1967, Bowman started the process of building the three-story North Shore Apartments on the property. (Courtesy of the Forest Lake Historical Society.)

Not much is known about Hanson's Resort on Clear Lake. In this 1938 photograph, a boat landing can be seen with a sign that reads, "No Fishing Off Landing." Hanson's was one of two boat rental services on the lake at the time, the other being Godfrey Peterson, who offered a large picnic area as well. (Courtesy of the Forest Lake Historical Society.)

SUNSHINE LODGE, FOREST LAKE, MINN. 0913

The Mary Davis Sunshine Lodge opened in 1906, just north of downtown Forest Lake. It was established for the purpose of providing relaxation and fun for children and their mothers with little means. Its benefactor, Mary J. Davis, was part of the Minnesota chapter of the International Sunshine Society and recognized the need for more access to open spaces. In nearby Lindström, a chapter was started in 1904 consisting of two small rental cottages, but the owner was about to sell. A cottage with two lots next to the grade school was secured and repairs were begun almost immediately. Forest Lake citizens poured their time and effort into providing all they could for the Sunshine Lodge and its visitors. It was relocated in the 1920s to the area of present-day Sunshine Court, named after the lodge. (Courtesy of the Forest Lake Historical Society.)

Stanley Tolberg smiles for the camera as he awaits the next big bite. Tolberg worked for the Forest Lake Oil Company that was owned by A.R. Lake. He later became a village trustee and village assessor, starting in 1948. His wife, Marian, was a teacher at Forest Lake Elementary. (Courtesy of Diane Knutson.)

More fishermen join Stanley Tolberg in this photograph; they are taking a break for some lunch. Not much has changed with ice fishing in 100 years besides some added creature comforts and improved technology. The simple icehouse shown here with its stove pipe coming out the top was enough to keep everyone warm. (Courtesy of Diane Knutson.)

In 1949, the Veterans of Foreign Wars decided to sponsor an ice fishing contest, which drew 1,429 fishermen to Forest Lake. This photograph, taken in 1950, shows the second annual contest. Each year, a different design was made on the ice. In 1950, the pattern chosen was a Maltese cross that was dyed red and blue and appeared in papers across the country. Subsequent patterns included a liberty bell, iron lung, and a Mexican sombrero. In 1950, the first prize was an all-expenses-paid vacation for one week in Mexico City and Acapulco. The winner was Hank Marcott of White Bear Lake, who caught a 6-pound, 12-ounce northern pike. The Jaycees took over the sponsorship soon after and carried it for the next 15 years. Forest Lake would eventually be home to one of the largest ice fishing contests in the nation. (Courtesy of the Forest Lake Historical Society.)

This photograph from the public bathing beach shows a more open view toward First Lake. The old railroad park had been leased to build a gas station in 1954, much to the chagrin of the townspeople. Eventually, commercial expansion forced the public park to be relocated to where it is today. (Courtesy of the Forest Lake Historical Society.)

This photograph from 1950 shows a more modern view of the boat landing, with outdoor lighting and a fleet of rowboats positioned in such a way that they appear to be defending the area. To capitalize on the tourist boom, speedboat rides were now being offered as well as trolling motors for a little extra. (Courtesy of the Forest Lake Historical Society.)

Eddie Shipstead of Ice Follies fame had a home on Forest Lake, seen in this 1942 photograph. He was born in St. Paul and joined brother Ray and friend Oscar Johnson in 1936 to start the touring ice show that would become known all over the country. It still exists today as Disney on Ice. Shipstead married Lulu Heim of Wyoming, Minnesota. (Courtesy of the Forest Lake Historical Society.)

This 1950 photograph may have been taken from the Shipstead home or next to it. The camera faces First Lake toward South Shore Drive. The lake was much quieter back then, and everything was in walking distance of this spot, just a block south of Broadway Avenue. (Courtesy of the Forest Lake Historical Society.)

This home was owned by Paul Bremer, brother to bank founder Otto Bremer. It is located at 668 Fifth Street SE on First Lake. When first built, the property encompassed everything north of South Shore Drive up to the lake. Around the time of their nephew's kidnapping by the Barker-Karpis gang, the family hired a local man by the name of Art Forsberg as a bodyguard. Grace Bremer insisted he carry a pistol to protect her two daughters. One day, her daughter, also named Grace, was swimming alone, and three ominous men in suits and fedoras were rowing a boat toward her. Realizing her daughter was not in the house, Mrs. Bremer rushed out with a gun and started shooting toward the men in the rowboat. She did not hit them, but they started rowing away as fast as they could. (Courtesy of the Forest Lake Historical Society.)

Six

DOWNTOWN

The Stille brothers arrived in the United States from Germany in 1869 and eventually made their way to Forest Lake. By the late 1800s, they owned a saloon (pictured) and a three-story hotel. When the hotel burned in 1899, this structure likely burned with it. After the hotel was rebuilt, the saloon was moved to the hotel. This building was near the southeast corner of Broadway Avenue and Lake Street. (Courtesy of the Minnesota Historical Society.)

Most photographers never bothered with the west side of downtown. The structures were few and mostly wooden. In contrast, the east side was lined with new brick buildings and had more eye appeal. Thus, this 1906 photograph offers a rare glimpse of the storefronts in that area. Leon Nadeau's Lunch Room, A.W. Johnson's Grocery, and J.P. Murphy's Hardware are just some of the businesses shown here. (Courtesy of the Minnesota Historical Society.)

This view from the north end of town shows the same group of buildings to the right. The photographer, John Bowers, took this photograph standing in the middle of the intersection of Lake Street and Second Avenue around 1906. Oscar Berggren's blacksmith shop is to the left. Just out of frame are the Presbyterian church (left) and city hall and schoolhouse (right). (Courtesy of the Minnesota Historical Society.)

VIEW ON MAIN ST FOREST LAKE MINN

This sweeping view of North Lake Street in 1906 shows the progress Forest Lake had made in the last several years. The massive brick building in the foreground was the new hardware store owned by David E. Young, who came to Forest Lake about the same year. Upstairs, the Modern Woodmen of America had a space called Woodmen Hall for its social gatherings. It was also the site of the town's first Catholic Mass in 1904, which continued until St. Peter's was built in 1905. The next owner was Frank R. Herzberg. He grew up in Paynesville, Minnesota, and started out in the grocery business. By 1910, he owned a hardware store in Claremont, Minnesota, and then took over Young's Hardware in 1917. He ran the business until 1946, when he sold it and the building to Lloyd and Lil Bergstrom. It would eventually become Carter's Jewelry and Gifts in 1964. The building was demolished in 1968. (Courtesy of the Forest Lake Historical Society.)

An abundance of beer signs lure thirsty patrons into the many saloons in Forest Lake's business district. In the foreground, P.T. Sullivan's Sample Room sold Golden Grain Belt beer. The two-story building in the background, Phil's Place, sold Hamm's. Saloons were required by law to be closed on Sundays. When Prohibition began, bar owners either changed their business or sold out. Looking to the left of the Sample Room is Lakeside Pharmacy, which may have been owned by Willard Walker. He and his brother Frank started a lumber company in Forest Lake in 1894 but seemed to have had multiple businesses at the time. In the 1900 census, Willard is listed as a "druggist." It is likely he had no formal training in pharmacology and sold mostly patent medicines, like Lydia Pinkham's Vegetable Compound, and other tonics and elixirs. (Courtesy of the Minnesota Historical Society.)

The Johnson & Shafer Ice Company wagon is shown hauling ice to customers on South Lake Street. In this photograph, it has stopped in front of Strange's Place. William Strange was a saloonkeeper from Montana who took over the business from P.T. Sullivan. He also ran a hotel and lunchroom in this same building. (Courtesy of the Forest Lake Historical Society.)

William Jackson Simmons was an early Forest Lake businessman, having opened one of the earliest general stores in town by the 1870s. Simmons also served as the town's first treasurer in 1875. His balance sheets were always complete and his handwriting impeccable. This photograph shows the inside of his general store in 1909. Simmons is standing on the right, looking very dapper. (Courtesy of LoraLee Briley.)

The A.E. Valenty Billiard Parlor was just north of Broadway Avenue and Lake Street on the east side. A familiar barber pole at right marks the location of John Grieman's barbershop. Grieman and his brother Joe started out in the corner of Valenty's parlor before moving into their own building. Both Valenty and Grieman were longtime businessmen in Forest Lake. (Courtesy of Bert and Elsie Vogel family.)

George Landgraver holds the horses' reins long enough for a photograph. His son George Jr. sits in front of him. The rest of the men are unidentified. This photograph was taken around 1919 and shows Landgraver taking his wagons to the Forest Lake Garage for possible wheel service or dropping off an order. He owned the Livery and Dray Line on Broadway Avenue and was a familiar sight in town. (Courtesy of Audrey Gemeiner.)

2017

MAIN STREET LOOKING NORTH, FOREST LAKE, MINN,

The group of children at left are likely walking to school, which was just a block north of downtown. In the foreground, the main street shows its true colors after an early morning rain. The buildings shown here have all been demolished except for a few in the far distance. The village water mains were laid in 1921, as evidenced by a fire hydrant on the corner. Businesses that can be seen here are Stille's Confectionery on the corner, Hurd's Land Office, Carl Heyne (tailor), and J.J. Swanson's grocery store. A.E. Valenty's billiard parlor does not have a sign but is to the left of Swanson's store. The look of downtown Forest Lake would be changed forever in 1926 when pavement went in. It had been installed in neighboring Hugo just a year prior. (Courtesy of Bert and Elsie Vogel family.)

J.L. Simmons and son Lawrence are standing at their place of business (at left). Johnson and Reioux Meat Market, F.C. Bergh's Drug Store, and the Forest Lake State Bank can also be seen. Most of the buildings here are still standing, with the exception of the drugstore and the large brick structure at the end. This photograph dates to around 1909. (Courtesy of the Forest Lake Historical Society.)

This 1913 photograph of the post office shows the first mail truck, complete with the Stars and Stripes on the side panel. A sign above the entryway announces the upcoming Washington County Fair. At far left is the Hotel Vexio, a precursor to the Commercial Hotel. The empty lot between them is the future site of the theater building. (Courtesy of the Otto Manke family.)

If there was ever a photograph to show how Forest Lake was progressing, this was it. Taken around 1918, there are new brick buildings, automobiles, and a street that almost looks groomed. In the new theater building, dentist Chester Dewert Larson has an office in a back room, a beginning to his practice that would last 53 years. He graduated from the University of Minnesota and opened his business in February 1917. At that time, an average tooth extraction was $1, and a full upper or lower denture was $15–25. Often, patients made payments in trade with potatoes, eggs, chickens, and vegetables. Dr. Larson eventually moved from the theater building to the Herzberg building a few structures south. He and Dr. Poirier shared the top floor. Dr. Larson would live to be 101 years old. (Courtesy of the Forest Lake Historical Society.)

Engquist Hardware was another staple of the community. Bill Engquist and his brother Vic started their business on South Lake Street in 1915. Vic had recently learned the plumbing trade from his previous employer, J.P. Murphy, who owned a hardware store on North Lake Street. The business opened every morning at 6:00 a.m. for the farmers and closed at twilight, when the streetlamps were lit. When electricity and running water came to Forest Lake, eager customers came to see the Engquists for their wiring and plumbing needs. The business was moved to North Lake Street a year after this photograph was taken in 1925. Engquist eventually sold his business in 1967 to Lester Matheson, who needed more room for his inventory. The hardware store was moved again to South Lake Street in a newer building that would become Hardware Hank, owned by Howard Ruggles. (Courtesy of Bert and Elsie Vogel family.)

By 1922, the post office moved a block south. German emigrant E.A. Preuss had recently moved from Wausau, Wisconsin, with his wife, Minnie. They decided to open a confectionery store in the old post office. Their business had barely been established when E.A. contracted tuberculosis and died in 1920. Minnie promptly took over, which is indicated on the awning, which reads "Mrs. E.A. Preuss." (Courtesy of the Forest Lake Historical Society.)

Two large gas pumps can be seen in front of the Carpenter Oil station on the left in this photograph from around 1924. The next business to the north was the J.B. Weisser Lumber Company, which took over Walker and Goodine's Lumber Yard in 1921. Weisser and his brother Frank operated the business for 40 years until selling in 1961 to the Salzer Lumber Company. (Courtesy of Bert and Elsie Vogel family.)

After L.P. Melbostad closed his grocery store on North Lake Street, he bought the Shell Oil station in April 1943 in the vicinity of Highway 61 and Northwest Third Avenue. It was later purchased by Pat Whitman and then Dan Nielsen in 1947, who changed the name to Dan's Phillips 66. (Courtesy of Sue Erickson.)

By the mid-1930s, the main street is barely recognizable from photographs 10 years earlier. Dirt has been replaced by pavement, and new buildings line the west side. With all the automobiles driving past, business signs act as modern-day billboards, capturing the attention of the driver with a few key words. Reub's Tire Shop can be easily seen here. (Courtesy of the Forest Lake Historical Society.)

The former saloon on the right was looking old and tired by 1938; a shaded area below the windows once held the sign for Golden Grain Belt Beers and others. Its brick neighbors, looking new and ornate, were built by local bricklayer Karl Levin. Many buildings up and down Lake Street were built by Levin; however, none exist today. The Chevrolet and Buick sign was at the Forest Lake Motor Company, which was owned by Cody Hoekstra. He also served as Forest Lake's mayor from 1943 to 1946. On the morning of October 3, 1946, a worker at Hoekstra's garage was using a welding torch, which set off a spark and ignited nearby oil and gasoline. Soon, a raging fire consumed the building and threatened the nearby Vogel's Hotel. The garage was a total loss, and the hotel suffered damage to its roof. (Courtesy of the Forest Lake Historical Society.)

Wagner's Hamburger Shop was a cornerstone of the Forest Lake community. Frank and Eva Wagner purchased the existing shop and turned it into a 24/7 burger joint. They even had slot machines, dice games, and pinball for customers to enjoy. During World War II, Eva collected photographs of all the servicemen in their uniforms and hung them on the walls of the restaurant. Frequent customers included fishermen and hunters who needed an early breakfast before going out. Inevitably, they would turn up again later in the day before heading home. Teenagers loved hanging out at Wagner's after dances and other school functions. Frank and Eva eventually sold their business to Eva's brother Herb Taurman and his wife, Keena. Son Buster took over the business sometime later. Some of the last owners were Tom and Norma Zschokke. Pictured here are Herb Taurman (left) and John Hehner. (Courtesy of Diane Knutson.)

Karl Levin's signature brickwork can be seen on the Wally's Café building in this 1942 photograph. The earliest record of a business in this spot shows Stille's Confectionery, which was eventually sold in 1927 to Wally and Marie Frederickson. Nick Mitsoff also had his photography studio in this building. (Courtesy of the Forest Lake Historical Society.)

The building on the far left is the Ed Johnson Electric Company. Johnson started his business in 1923 and sold it in the early 1950s. The Commercial Hotel building to its right diversified and added a bowling alley in the basement, which created many jobs for the local teenagers as pinsetters. This photograph is from 1946. (Courtesy of the Forest Lake Historical Society.)

At left, the Forest Lake Dairy Store (also known as Cara-Van Dairy), shown in 1950, was a popular stop for Russell's Ice Cream, which was made in Superior, Wisconsin. Ice cream cones after Sunday church services were a particularly cherished memory of local youngsters. A café also served breakfast and lunch as well as egg coffee all day. (Courtesy of the Forest Lake Historical Society.)

Lyle Morehead opened Red Owl on July 1, 1946. After nine years, it moved to the former Pepin Oil Company building near the south end of North Lake Street. In 1964, the building was remodeled. Five years later, it moved again into a new building on the old Salzer Lumber lot just north of there. In 1977, it became Johnson's Super Valu. (Courtesy of the Forest Lake Historical Society.)

This 1950 view looking south on North Lake Street shows an RV park to the right, next to the old village hall. Years before, it was a tourist camp for visitors with tall, shady trees and a spacious lawn. Before that, Forest Lake's first school was built in the village hall spot in 1874 and served as the location for town meetings. It later burned in 1913. The Mary Davis Sunshine Lodge was first located next to the school before it moved to the area of present-day Sunshine Court. To the left, Erickson's gas station can be seen, along with the Pure Oil station. In the distance is a bustling downtown scene. The stores have unfurled their awnings to shade against the morning sun. It is a beautiful day in Forest Lake. (Courtesy of the Forest Lake Historical Society.)

When Bert and Elsie Vogel opened Skateland on June 17, 1955, it ushered in a period that would be remembered by residents young and old for the rest of their lives. It was often described as a "home away from home" and a good place to burn off energy for less than a buck. On Saturday mornings, the line to the counter would start to build with people waiting for skates and looking around for friends. Once out on the floor, there were calls for "crack the whip" or "snowball." Some would show off their balancing skills with "shoot the duck." The Vogels also held costume parties and hosted school proms. Every March, Elsie would start planning the annual Skateland Coronation and Skating Show—an event with over 100 skaters. After 13 years, Bert and Elsie hung up the roller skates for good. They closed on September 30, 1968. It would remain closed until Patty Sietz reopened the business under the same name in 1977; however, it closed again in 1985. (Courtesy of Irene Arth.)

Del Larson (left) carries on a conversation while Elsie Vogel ties up her skates. Skateland is decorated for Halloween in this 1956 photograph. On the window, a sign advertises roller skating lessons at $2.50 for five lessons. Pop and candy were readily available behind the counter. (Courtesy of Irene Arth.)

Harold Moen opened his shoe store on March 1, 1956, near the southeast corner of North Lake Street and Second Avenue NW. Destroyed by fire in 1970, it reopened the following spring. Moen brought his sons Gary and Craig into the business in the 1970s and stayed until it closed in 1992. (Courtesy of Craig Moen.)

Vogel's café, hotel, and bar stood on the southeast corner of Broadway Avenue and Lake Street. At first, the Vogels leased Hendrickson's Café, the prior business in that building. In 1945, they decided to buy the business and make the name change. In the late 1950s, it was changed to Vogel's Supper Club. Fire claimed the iconic structure in 1963. (Courtesy of the Forest Lake Historical Society.)

This view is looking north from South Lake Street around 1955. All the familiar names can be seen—Vogel's, Wally's, Russell's, etc. Rows of streetlamps have replaced the old gas lanterns. Near the Times building is a large fundraising thermometer sign, which indicates how much money had been raised for the new District Memorial Hospital. (Courtesy of the Forest Lake Historical Society.)

Seven

FOURTH OF JULY

The Forest Lake American Legion, Post No. 225, has been leading the town's Fourth of July festivities for nearly 100 years. This very early program from 1927 promises a day filled with everything from popularity contests to dances and fireworks. Mayor Frank A. Johnson encouraged visitors to make use of Forest Lake's four up-to-date tourist camps free of charge. (Courtesy of the Forest Lake Historical Society.)

This photograph, taken on July 4, 1925, shows a band walking north on South Lake Street. This is thought to be the Interstate Band from Chisago County. The band was formed in the early 1900s and had similar uniforms. They were a mainstay in Forest Lake parades through the 1980s. The road is still dirt here and appears to have been groomed before the parade began. Pavement was added the following year. In the background is the Park Café building, which served "home cooking," as the sign reads. The Lake View Dairy building can also be seen. The parade route changed several times over the years but was mostly concentrated on Broadway Avenue and Lake Street. This photograph shows just a few spectators watching the band. Today, residents need to put chairs out to mark their spots before the sun comes up. (Courtesy of Diane Knutson.)

The Modern Woodmen of America was one of Forest Lake's most active organizations at the turn of the 20th century. They had a hall on the second floor of the Herzberg building for gatherings, and even had a band. Their parade float made of logs was always a familiar sight. (Courtesy of the Forest Lake Historical Society.)

The Forest Lake Oil Company float waits its turn in line before the parade starts. Owner Ran Lake is on the right. The man at left is unidentified. Parade floats were once a point of pride for business owners but are hardly seen today. In the background, the first jail building can be seen as well as the first town hall. (Courtesy of Diane Knutson.)

This very early photograph of a parade float was taken when cars did not yet have the power to pull such a load. The float seen here was not as imaginative as a sailing ship but was still very decorative for its day. It is difficult to tell what business or organization it represented. (Courtesy of Diane Knutson.)

This parade photograph from the 1920s or 1930s clearly shows a float made to look like a boat. The wording on the side reads, "Our Town is Yours Today." Visitors came from all over to see Forest Lake's parade, and its citizens were always eager to show outsiders their hospitality. (Courtesy of Diane Knutson.)

For the first time ever, Forest Lake had three different parades in 1948. The first was on July 3, which featured the draft horse parade seen here. The second was on July 4, which was the majorette parade. The state championship baton twirling contest was in Forest Lake that week. Last was the regular parade on July 5. In this photograph, the American Legion leads the parade on horseback, with a line of horses following. It is surprising to see so few spectators. J.B. Weisser, who was known for always having a cigar in his hand, may be the man at the door on the left smoking a cigar outside his office. The photographer is likely standing on top of the building to get this shot. (Courtesy of the Forest Lake Historical Society.)

An unidentified marching band heads down South Lake Street in this 1960 parade. Crowds seem to be more abundant by this time, lining both sides of the street. In the background is Vogel's Supper Club and Wally's Café to the north. The view of this corner changed forever when a fire claimed the Vogel building in 1963. (Courtesy of Greg Mackey.)

Neil "Bud" Robinson had a striking resemblance to Kentucky Fried Chicken's spokesman, Colonel Sanders. He was always a highlight of the Forest Lake parade, waving his hat to onlookers with one hand and eating a chicken drumstick with the other. This photograph dates from the late 1960s. (Courtesy of Corliss Vadner.)

It is not known when the Forest Lake Marching Band first formed. The earliest records show a marching band in the early 1940s. Band teacher Rollie Nelson took over in the late 1940s and stayed on as director until the summer of 1976. The marching band was very successful in the 1960s and participated in a national competition in New York in 1965. There were various directors for the next several years until band teacher Richard Hahn took over in the fall of 1980. The marching band stayed active through the late 1990s and was eventually disbanded. It returned in 2016 under the direction of Jake Matheson. This photograph was taken in the summer of 1979. Banner carriers were Cheryl Esberg (left) and Sue Skoglund. At far left, a new restaurant, Der Lach Haus, stands in place of Vogel's Supper Club. (Courtesy of Sue Ruggles-Coy.)

The Fourth of July parade was not all about floats and marching bands. Sometimes it involved cross-dressing men on skis drinking beer. In this parade photograph from 1979, five men turn some heads with their creativity as they make their way down South Lake Street. (Courtesy of the Forest Lake Historical Society.)

Shantell Paul is crowned Little Miss Forest Lake in this 1979 parade photograph. There was also a Miss Forest Lake pageant that began in 1939 and lasted until 1980. This was one of the few years when the Forest Lake Fire Department had to leave the parade to put out a house fire. (Courtesy of the Forest Lake Historical Society.)

The Forest Lake City Marching Band was formed by Forest Lake High School alumni Steve Hursh and Brian Tolzmann in 1981. The group was directed by Rollin Nelson, who had just retired from teaching high school band for many years. The group went on to become a seven-time state champion, a six-time Midwest region champion, and the 1985 national champion in open class band categories. During a 1985 broadcast, NBC television personality Willard Scott called the band the best he had ever seen. This 1981 photograph was taken in the inaugural year, with band members wearing matching black and white caps as they march down North Lake Street. At top right, business owner Harold Moen stands outside his shoe store with his arms folded, enjoying the music. He played in the high school band during its early days. (Courtesy of Faith Lutheran Church.)

The German Sitting Band debuted at the 1968 Forest Lake Diamond Jubilee Parade. It was originally called Duke's Mixture Band because of all the nationalities of its members. However, only German music was played. From left to right are (backs turned) Neil Mattson, Larry Patak, and Dr. Carl Peikert; (facing camera) Steve Hursh, Bill Butler, Bud Robinson (conducting with a plunger), and Leonard Tolzmann. (Courtesy of Corliss Vadner.)

In this early 1980s parade photograph, two Hardware Hank inflatable men walk down South Lake Street. Howard Ruggles was the owner of Hardware Hank, located behind the photographer. In the background, the E.J. Houle Grain Elevator towers above the city skyline. (Courtesy of Sue Ruggles-Coy.)

About the Forest Lake Historical Society

The first attempt at creating a local historical museum was in 1949 with the celebration of the town's diamond jubilee. Historical artifacts and photographs were brought in from all over, and it was soon apparent that a story needed to be told. An article in the *Forest Lake Times* Diamond Jubilee Edition read, "The iron is hot at this very moment—may never again be as hot. History is in the air around Forest Lake, and old-timers realize more than ever before that they are in a position to contribute greatly and quite tangibly to the recording and perpetuating of things historical." Unfortunately, the iron quickly cooled, and nothing more was done.

In 2011, a group of volunteers gathered to create a temporary historical museum to promote interest within the community. It was not long before donations started to pour in, sending a signal that a more permanent organization was needed to collect, preserve, and share the history of the Forest Lake area. The following year, the Forest Lake Area Historical Society was created. In 2019, a separate and more focused historical society was created to meet the demand for Forest Lake history that was being generated on the Facebook group Old Forest Lake, started by resident Justin Brink.

The Forest Lake Historical Society is a 501(c)(3) organization that was formed exclusively for the purpose of the collection, preservation, and dissemination of historical knowledge about the Forest Lake area. The website is www.forestlakehistory.org. Questions or other inquiries may be emailed to forestlakehistory@gmail.com.

DISCOVER THOUSANDS OF LOCAL HISTORY BOOKS FEATURING MILLIONS OF VINTAGE IMAGES

Arcadia Publishing, the leading local history publisher in the United States, is committed to making history accessible and meaningful through publishing books that celebrate and preserve the heritage of America's people and places.

Find more books like this at
www.arcadiapublishing.com

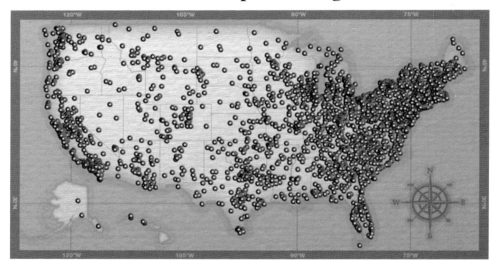

Search for your hometown history, your old stomping grounds, and even your favorite sports team.

Consistent with our mission to preserve history on a local level, this book was printed in South Carolina on American-made paper and manufactured entirely in the United States. Products carrying the accredited Forest Stewardship Council (FSC) label are printed on 100 percent FSC-certified paper.

MADE IN THE USA